The Cormorant and the Clam

Based on
A True Story

Written by Consie Berghausen
Illustrated by Nina Berghausen

Riverhaven Books

Published in the United States by
Riverhaven Books, Massachusetts.

ISBN 978-1-937588-57-1

Printed in the United States of America
by Country Press, Lakeville, Massachusetts

Designed by Stephanie Lynn Blackman
Whitman, MA

Dedicated to my husband and
daughter, Nina,
whose adventure inspired this story

Nina and Dad are ready to ride.
In their kayak, they paddle and glide
From the saltwater marsh to the sea,
Rowing together so happily.
Out for just a midday excursion,
Hoping to find seaside diversion.

They slide through the marsh in their red kayak,
Passing bushes of beach rose and lilac.
It's high tide so their craft won't run aground
Near grassy backyards where kids run around.

They steer from Buck's Creek
    out toward Ridgevale Beach.
Nina paddles and listens
        to Dad teach.

She learns about water currents and tides.
This is a fun and a new learning ride.
Nina looks up where birds fly so regal;
Dad calls out, "There's a heron and seagull."

Once they arrive they find people galore,
Some swim, some sail, others play on the shore.
Sun-tanning friends recline up on warm sand,
Each having fun on this beachy Cape land.

Nina and Dad sit facing the ocean,
Then Dad observes an odd commotion.
Wings are flapping: it's a cormorant beached!
He's not moving well so Dad runs to reach
The bird to find what the trouble might be.
Nina follows along and they both see…

The cormorant swinging his head around,
He's flailing, rubbing his face on the ground.
There seems to be something stuck on his beak,
They creep in closer for a better peek.

A quahog clam is clamped on the bird's nose.
That's not where a quahog ever should go!
Maybe the bird wanted a tasty treat,
Nipped at the clam, but was thoroughly beat.

With beak shut snug, the bird can't eat or drink;
He's weak from hunger, so Dad wisely thinks.
"Nina, we must pull that clam off of him.
We have to catch him, but where to begin?"

Nina circles round, Dad quickly pounces;
He grabs the cormorant as it flounces.
Dad is fast and gives the quahog a tug.
It's stuck on firmly, and that clam won't budge.

Dad tries again, but the clam is stuck tight.
The bird doesn't move, motionless from fright.
First a clam clamped snug onto his poor beak,
Leaving him unable to drink or eat,
Now a giant man is grabbing at him,
There's no place to run and nowhere to swim.

Nina says, "Dad, we must take him back home;"
Dad nods and pins the wings so he can't roam.
Back in their kayak, they shove off to sea,
Wondering what strategy there might be.

They need a good tool to pry off the clam;
Nina paddles and glides as fast as she can
Through the marsh until they land at their yard,
Dad runs for the shed while Nina stands guard.

A screwdriver, of course, Dad hopes will work.
Cormorant wiggles, he's thoroughly irked.
Off the clam flies; the bird's finally free.
Surely he's happy as happy can be.

They step back and wait for the bird to fly.
Instead, he turns and looks Dad in the eye,
Lifts into the air, stretches his neck,
Poops on Dad's leg, gives Dad's head a hard peck.

Though he's ungrateful for his lucky day,
The cormorant flaps his wings to away.
Dad and Nina are stunned, words can't be found,
Then both start laughing and fall on the ground.

This memory made, they're glad they could see
The cormorant and the clam be set free.

Please visit www.ConsieBerghausen.com
to learn more about her stories,
to download worksheets, and to see what both
author and illustrator are working on next.

www.ingramcontent.com/pod-product-compliance
Lightning Source LLC
Chambersburg PA
CBHW060833270326
41933CB00002B/72